Angels and Dragons: Faces at St Ma Virgin, Bottesford

Neil Fortey and Robert Sparham

Bottesford Community Heritage Project

Published: 2014

ISBN: 978-0-9570631-7-4

Photographs © Neil Fortey & Kate Pugh, 2013

Illustrations from British Library (open source), the Dean and Chapter of Westminster, and courtesy of Bottesford Parochial Church Council.

Printed by Russell Press Ltd, Russell House, Bulwell Lane, Nottingham NG6 0BT

This book has been created as part of the Bottesford Community Heritage Project, a not-for-profit group of volunteers studying the history of the parish of Bottesford and Muston, Leicestershire.

Foreword

I am pleased to recommend this book to all readers. 'Angels and Dragons' provides a fascinating guide to the stone carvings inside and outside St Marys, Bottesford. The photographs and narrative by Neil and Bob are particularly informative and are a welcome addition to the history of St Marys. The book provides an insight into the development of religious beliefs in past times and a reference for future generations.

The Bottesford Community Heritage Project has kindly offered to donate part of the proceeds from this volume to the Friends of St Marys, who are dedicated to the preservation of this wonderful building and its contents. We are eternally grateful.

John Daybell,

Chairman, Friends of St Marys, Bottesford

Cover pictures:

The front cover picture shows a face mounted on the eastern end of the south clerestory.

The rear cover picture is of a crudely carved face that stares from the stones inside the porch. Its age is uncertain, but may be early 19th Century. Stone benches in the porch bear graffiti outlines of workmen's shoes, and similar shoe outlines that were also inscribed into the roof lead bear early 19th Century dates.

Contents

Introduction

Churches and cathedrals display a host of images of faces, realistic and allegorical, in statues, gargoyles and grotesques, tombs and memorials, floor-brasses and stained glass. In addition to Jesus, Saints and biblical scenes, we meet church benefactors and innumerable anonymous carvings, sacred and profane. Men and women mix with angels and figures of evil. This book examines the variety of late-medieval and post-Reformation faces in one parish church in the East Midlands. St Mary the Virgin, Bottesford, is best known for the memorials of the Earls and Countesses of Rutland, but it also contains many other faces. Some are remarkable, all are interesting. Together they reflect the history of this corner of the country as well as the rich skills of the artist-craftsmen who created them.

St Mary's, the "Lady of the Vale", is at the heart of the most northerly parish of Leicestershire, a finger of land wedged between Nottinghamshire and Lincolnshire. Its spire, 210 feet high (64 m), is a landmark in the low-lying farmlands of the Vale of Belvoir. Visitors to the church are inevitably drawn to its chancel, packed with monuments of importance both as works of art and as a record of Tudor and Jacobean England. They may also look at the carvings of allegorical beasts at the tops of columns in the nave, but few will have lingered over carvings hiding in the darkness of the aisles and in the height of the clerestory, save perhaps for the carving of the sinner with his tongue and eye being eaten by a two-headed serpent seen in the north aisle.

There is much to look at: a Jacobean pulpit, a Tudor font (another in the Lady Chapel is said to be Anglo-Saxon), a 13th Century piscina, and next to the organ shallow niches where a side altar once stood. There are Victorian stained-glass windows and one window with reclaimed medieval stained-glass. There is the village War Memorial and around the walls of the aisles and chancel numerous memorial plaques and a series of heraldic hatchments.

St Mary the Virgin, "The Lady of the Vale"

Outside, gargoyles project from tower and aisle. Approaching the south porch, you can't miss two beautifully realistic gargoyles mounted on the south transept, popularly known as the 'Bellman' (or 'Tollman') and 'Alewife', seeming to welcome us to the market and to the church ale. There are many other carvings on the outside, faces on the aisles and transepts, faces crowded along the frieze round the parapet of the tower, arrays of figures sprouting from the clerestory. A pair of binoculars will help.

St Mary's stands at the centre of a sprawling farming parish, part of the old Danelaw where place names indicate communities of Scandinavians, as well as the Anglo-Saxons. There were originally three or more townships within Bottesford parish. In 1795, John Nichols recorded that there had been a church (more correctly, a chapelry) at Normanton, where the priest from St Mary's once held services three days a week, but which had already disappeared before his time. In 1845, local antiquary, Andrew Esdaile, mentioned other township churches at Bottesford "opposite the Rutland Arms" and also at Easthorpe and 'Wimbishthorpe', and also stated that St Mary's itself is on the site of Beckingthorpe old church. These assertions are hard to prove, in the absence of archaeological records. In any case, it was clearly St Mary's that prospered and achieved the status of a parish church where local people married, christened their children and buried their dead (and paid their tithes).

An 18th century engraving of St Mary's, Bottesford.

Bottesford was part of the estates of Belvoir. Its church has benefitted from the patronage of the lords of Belvoir from the 11th Century to the present day. Robert de Todeni was the Norman overlord, and a priest is recorded at Bottesford in the Domesday Book. The first recorded rector, Nicholas d'Albini, installed in 1209, was the youngest son of William d'Albini III of Belvoir, one of the barons who confronted King John at Runnymede in 1215.

Major rebuilding and enlargement of St Mary's commenced in the 14th Century, when Bottesford was the fourth largest settlement in Leicestershire, and continued in the 15th Century. This all took place during the lordship of the Barons de Roos. Their distinctive "Three Water-Bougets" arms are on the southern spandrel of the west door, on the sills of the empty niches on the south transept (now faint, due to centuries of weathering) and flamboyantly above the eastern pier of the north arcade, opposite the effigy of Bishop John Marshall of Llandaff, who was also a member of a prominent Bottesford family. Nichols recounted that the northern side of the nave is "ascribed" to the de Roos, the southern side to the Marshalls. St Mary's has served the needs of its patrons as well as those of parishioners to the present day, while the modest chapelries or chantries in the other townships in the parish struggled and finally expired. The funeral of the 10th Duke of Rutland was held at St Mary's in January, 1999.

In this book we look at the variety of carvings and other decorations in the church, from the truly grotesque to quite extraordinarily lifelike, of people and creatures. We have tried to bring out the way that the treatment of faces, in particular, changed over the centuries from late-Medieval to post-Reformation and then into the 19th century. Materials have also evolved, from the pinkish grey limestone of the medieval work, through the alabaster and marble of the Tudor and Jacobean, to Victorian and Medieval stained glass. There are remains of a Doom painted on the plaster-covered wall above the chancel arch. There are examples of a medieval floor-brass in the chancel.

We have added a commentary on the history and significance of the carvings, relating them to the development of the building itself and its relationship to the broader historic and cultural setting. Many carvings on parish churches in general are allegorical, with recurrent themes such as the 'green man'. At Bottesford there is a more noticeable emphasis on realism in the faces in the Medieval carvings. They span the period from the early 14th Century to shortly before the Reformation. It can be argued that the effigies on the post-Reformation tombs continue this evolution towards greater realism, portraying the identity and piety of the deceased, rather than the object of his

A benign angelic face on the transverse arch at the eastern end of the south aisle .

The Bellman (or Tollman, the man who tolled the bell on market day) and the Alewife look out from the south transept.

faith and devotion. The figures on the tombs are remarkably life-like. It's as if we are witnessing stages by which the Renaissance reached the parish, followed by the Baroque of the later, 17th Century tombs, or put more simply, we see the passage from the Medieval world to the modern world.

This is not intended to be an exhaustive survey. We want to focus as much on the beauty of the images as the history they have to tell. We have been again and again deeply impressed by the skill and artistry of the medieval masons and painters, and of the later sculptors and creators of stained glass, whose work is so abundantly displayed. Most are anonymous, especially where pre-Reformation work is involved, yet there are great artistic and craftsman skills on display. Today they would be celebrated artists and deservedly honoured. With the later work, the names of the alabaster and marble sculptors are known in many cases, as are those of the creators of the 19th Century stained glass windows.

However, it must be emphasised that St Mary's is not a museum or an art gallery. It is a living building where the art is put there for a variety of purposes, but never just because it is beautiful. Most of all, of course, it is a parish church, a place where the community has worshipped for hundreds of years, and long may it continue to do so.

Acknowledgements

This book is a contribution to the Bottesford Community Heritage Project, and also to the fund-raising of the Friend's of St Mary's. The idea for it came from the photographic recording of figurative carvings at St Mary's as a contribution to Project Gargoyle, the recording of figurative carvings in Leicestershire churches led by Bob Trubshaw on behalf of Leicestershire County Council. Much of Project Gargoyle is carried out by volunteers. It has been a 'learning experience', prompting questions of when and why the carvings were created. Leicestershire has a wealth of such art, often overlooked by historians. Our aim has been to put the outcome of our part of Project Gargoyle to work, reproducing a selection of the images to prompt discussion of what they are and why they are there.

This book follows on from the Bottesford Living History Project (2006 to 2009), which was funded by the former Local Heritage Initiative (Countryside Agency) and managed by the Heritage Lottery Fund (Grant LH-06-086). The outcome of this project was published as "Not Forgetting: Aspects of Village Life in Bottesford, Easthorpe, Muston and Normanton", Bottesford Community Heritage Project, 2009.

We are grateful for the support of the Friends of St Mary's, Bottesford, who encouraged preparation of a small exhibition in the church of some of these pictures in 2012. We are grateful to churchwarden John Topps for his help, which included generously allowing access to the otherwise security-protected church roofs one fine day in 2012. We are grateful to Michael Saunders for sharing his knowledge and enthusiasm, and showing us the list of the church windows and their makers, for the information given by Dr. Madelaine Grey of the University of Wales with regard to the association of St Mary's with Bishop Marshall of Llandaff, to Evan McWilliam of the University of York regarding the age of the font, and to the Dean and Chapter of Westminster

We acknowledge extracting details from the church guidebooks, one published in 1972 by M.P.Dare, and a later one written by the E.A. (Ted) Shipman, c.1990, followed in 1995 by his *Gleanings from St Mary's*. None are in press, though a modern revision of the 1990 guidebook is available at the church. We are grateful to Lionel Wall for sharing his findings and thoughts, to Catherine Pugh for constant support and critical advice, and to Kathy Sparham, John Daybell, Shirley Daybell and Sue Dunsmore for spotting errors and making improvements to the text.

Francis Manners, the 2nd son of Francis, 6th Earl of Rutland, who died in 1620 allegedly of witchcraft.

INTERIOR OF BOTTESFORD CHURCH, LEICESTERSHIRE.

A 19th century engraving of the interior of St Mary's, Bottesford, looking westwards from the high altar.

6

Historic Framework

Looking around this beautiful church there is, perhaps, a tendency to think it so well-proportioned and matched that it must all have been planned and built at the same time. This impression, though natural, is quite misleading; the church was built in several stages. In 1795, John Nichols described St Mary's, giving details which include a list of the stained glass in the clerestory which was subsequently removed during 19th Century 'restoration', but saying nothing about carvings other than the tombs in the chancel. Sir Nikolaus Pevsner published a typically concise description, stating in broad terms when different parts were built, but hardly mentions the imagery apart from the chancel monuments. The description in the Listed Building record [*www.britishlistedbuildings.co.uk*] provides a summary of the chronology, but again gives only the most sparing of attention to the carvings. There are descriptions in church guidebooks by M.P. Dare and E.A. Shipman, but neither say much about the medieval imagery. This is an important matter when we seek to put the medieval work into a time sequence: we will say how we see the history of the building.

In pre-Reformation times the interior of St Mary's, like other English churches, would have been richly coloured, its sculpture vividly so, its walls brightly painted with religious scenes, images and patterns. There was a rood screen and loft with statues of the Crucifixion, St Mary and St John. There were three chantries and a Lady Chapel. Radical change took place during the Reformation and Civil War, c.1538-1660. The rood loft and devotional images were removed, the chantries dissolved, and the internal arrangements underwent major changes. Painted plaster was stripped and the interior became plain and sober. The bare stonework interior seen today resulted from further 19th Century removal of even the plain plaster. The Medieval carvings that remain represent merely a part of what was a colourful scheme whose subtlety and complexity we can only speculate about. They are survivors.

In the north aisle, we encounter this macabre figure, beautifully carved in what may be Purbeck stone, in contrast to the pale pinkish grey stone of the arches themselves. The dragon's claws, scales and two heads, tormenting the liar, are very detailed.

Plan of St Mary's - *taken from the drawing displayed in the south aisle, which has the words: National Silver Medal Drawings: Cecil A.L. Sutton from "The Building News" April 3, 1908.*

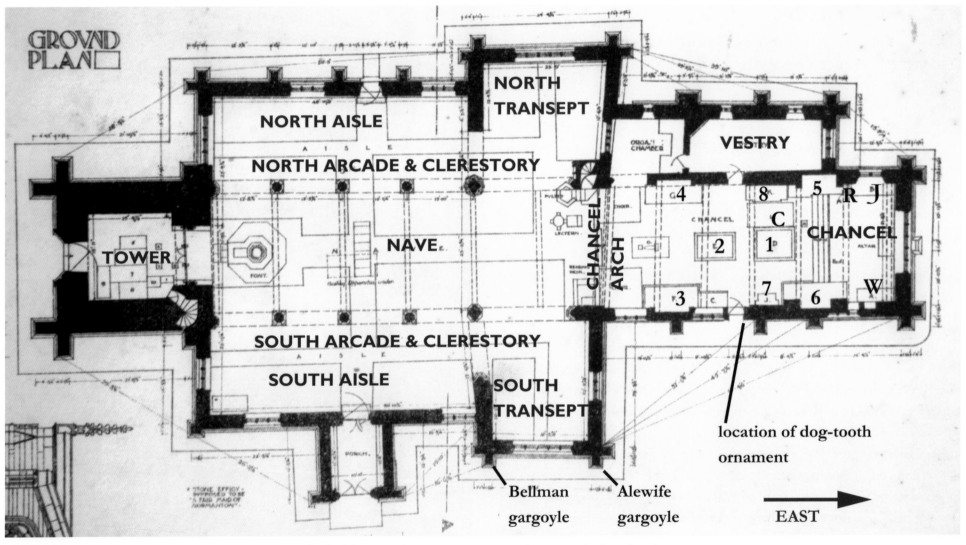

Key to the Tombs and effigies:

C - Henry de Coddyngton brass

R - effigy of Sir Robert de Roos

W - tomb of Sir William de Roos

J - tomb of Sir John de Roos

1 - tomb, 1st Earl of Rutland

2 - tomb, 2nd Earl of Rutland

3 - tomb, 3rd Earl of Rutland

4 - tomb, 4th Earl of Rutland

5 - tomb, 5th Earl of Rutland

6 - tomb, 6th Earl of Rutland

7 - tomb, 7th Earl of Rutland

8 - tomb, 8th Earl of Rutland

The changes went further. The resplendent alabaster and marble tombs of eight successive earls and their ladies of the Manners family, together with Medieval effigy and tombs of members of the de Roos family, dominate the chancel. The effect is that of a spectacularly theatrical mausoleum, and it is this that most visitors come to see.

St Mary's has a deceptively simple plan. The nave is flanked by north and south aisles, the tower at its western end. Chancel, north chancel aisle, transepts and south porch complete an overall cruciform layout. However, there have been several stages of building and modification.

The chancel, of local Liassic ironstone, contains remnants of Early English architecture. In its southern wall there is part of a respond with 'dog-tooth' decoration and a capital, together with a fragmentary trace of a probable gothic arch. These have been interpreted as part of a southern aisle, though it is also possible that they may be remains of an external doorway. An Early English piscina is seen in the SE corner of the chancel. Ironstone masonry, probably also of the 13th Century, is seen in the north transept and a small patch in the wall of the north chancel aisle. The northern chancel wall retains two Early English arches which once gave access to a north chancel aisle.

The chancel has been considerably modified, windows inserted, a clerestory added and its northern aisle remodelled as a late Perpendicular vestry. In the southern wall are three square-topped Perpendicular windows, and above them a clerestory with close-spaced, square-framed Tudor windows. Some of the windows were blanked out when the huge tomb of the 6th Earl was emplaced early in the 17th Century. The chancel has a Perpendicular eastern window, and its northern wall has a Decorated window at its eastern end, with a small 'Tudor' window above it. The chancel aisle was replaced by the present two-story vestry, with its small arched and square-topped windows. The vestry served as the 17th Century village school, long before it acquiring its

Window in the south aisle, east of the porch; the right-hand side abuts against the stonework of the reconstructed south transept.

modern role as the benefice office. Old rooflines seen in the eastern wall of the nave record the steeply pitched chancel and nave roofs that were replaced by the present gently pitched roofs hidden by the parapets.

Other parts of the church are faced in Middle Jurassic oolitic-limestone ashlar, though cruder masonry is seen for instance internally where walls would be dimly lit and hidden by plaster and paint. The windows in the south aisle display curvilinear Decorated gothic tracery of the early 14th Century. The porch is also of this age, with small Decorated windows in its upper level indicating that there was once a 1st floor room (a parvaise): the Perpendicular external doorway is too high to accommodate the floor of this chamber, which may have been removed before the doorway was inserted.

The south transept was rebuilt in the Perpendicular style which is also seen in the clerestory above the nave. Inside you can see the junction between older walling contiguous with the south aisle and the new walling of the transept. The gable of the transept has a Perpendicular window flanked by statue niches (both empty) and gargoyles, above which is an ornate parapet and pinnacles. Windows in the north nave aisle belong to the Perpendicular, including two with square-topped shapes. The window inserted in the north transept is also Perpendicular.

The six-stage tower and recessed spire were built after the aisles, also in the Perpendicular style. At the top of the tower is a battlemented parapet with kiosks at the corners. Younger than the tower is the Perpendicular clerestory over the nave, which abuts against the tower. Here, rows of windows, eleven on either side, are accompanied by ornate parapets and pinnacles, together with the rows of carved figures pictured in later pages.

A late Medieval flourish is the decoration of the nave, in that the arcades are embellished with carvings of mythical beasts, together with heraldic shields and the figures of a king and a lady (or priest). These appear to date from the end of the 15th century, as discussed later, but it is doubtful if other major changes took place at this time. Later still, during or after the Reformation, were the building of the vestry, addition of the chancel clerestory and

The north transept window, Perpendicular style, but the carved faces at the label-stops may be later.

The western window of the north aisle, late-Perpendicular style, with contemporary carvings of faces at the label-stops.

construction of crypts under the sanctuary and vestry.

Based on this discussion, the history of the church that we propose is as follows:

Late 12th or 13th Century – an Early-English gothic church was erected. There may have been an Anglo-Saxon church at Bottesford and conceivably a Norman building: a priest is recorded in the Domesday Book (1086). However, the first recorded rector of Bottesford, installed in 1209, was Nicholas d'Albini, son of Baron William d'Albini III. In 1247, the lordship of Belvoir passed to the de Roos ('de Ros' or 'Ross') family when Sir Robert de Roos, whose effigy and Heartstone can be seen in St Mary's, married the heiress Isabel d'Albini. The de Roos already held large estates in Holderness and the Vale of Pickering that had come to them through the marriage of Peter de Ros to Adeline, the sister of Walter d'Espec (died 1153), builder of Helmsley Castle, Rievaulx Abbey, Kirkham Priory and Warden Abbey. Nevertheless, Belvoir must have been a valuable addition.

Early 14th Century – construction, using limestone ashlar, of the south aisle in the Decorated style. This was a time of prosperity and population increase in England. It may be that the Barons de Roos, or the local community, wished to re-fashion their parish church to accommodate a growing congregation and, perhaps, as a matter of pride and prestige.

Late 14th Century to early 15th Century – a period during which there was further enlargement, with construction of the north aisle and then the building of the tower and spire. This may have been intended to complete earlier work interrupted by the famines, Black Death and later plagues that beset the 14th Century. It was a time of widespread church building, out of piety and the need for penitence, and to reflect the sense of renewal and deliverance from what had been a truly awful series of events. Prosperity

Early 14th Century carvings in the south aisle: a bishop's face on the transverse arch at the end of the aisle.

based on the wool trade had returned to many parts of England, prompting the widespread building or expansion of churches, including as it seems St Mary's.

Mid-15th Century to Early 16th Century – The middle part of the 15th Century saw further enlargement and embellishment of St Mary's, with construction of the clerestory over the nave and reconstruction of the south transept. This may have been an optimistic time in Bottesford. The market cross is attributed to this period, suggesting moves to develop the village's commercial potential, and the work on the church can be seen as also expressing a mood of confidence. The Barons de Roos were prominent Lancastrian supporters. For instance, John the 7th Baron had fought at Agincourt (1415). However, their 'reign' ended abruptly, if temporarily, in 1461 when Thomas the 9th Baron was attainted by Edward IV, who went on to reward William Lord Hastings for his loyalty with extensive lands and castles including Belvoir. Hastings neglected the castle and used it as a source of materials for new building work in his preferred castle at Ashby de la Zouch. It seems likely therefore that Edward IV's reign saw a decline in Bottesford's fortunes, with little work taking place on the church at this time.

The carvings of fantastical beasts seen in the nave arcade are probably part of the mid-15th Century work, but the accompanying shields bearing the arms of the de Roos and the arms and effigy of Bishop Marshall of Llandaff may have been added later. John Marshall died in 1495. His will states that he was a native of Bottesford and that he bequeathed funds to establish a chantry at St Mary's. The Marshall shield is probably a late 15th Century addition perhaps related to a chantry in the south transept where the Lady Chapel is today.

The date of the Roos shield seems more problematical. The lack of quartering of the de Roos arms with those of the baroness's family may indicate that it commemorates a bachelor lord rather than Baron Thomas, whose wife was a member of the powerful Tiptoft and Charlton families. During the first year of Henry VII's reign (1485-86), Baron Thomas's exiled son, Edmund de Roos,

At the first springer of the south aisle arcade, a face in ecstasy, eyes uplifted.

petitioned successfully for the return of his family's estates and titles, but Edmunds years as the 10th Baron did not run smoothly. In 1492 an extraordinary Act of Parliament, reported by Nichols, stated that Edmund was *"not of sufficient discretion to guide himself and his livelihood"*, and deprived him of the right to manage his affairs, placing his brother-in-law Sir Thomas Lovell in charge. It is tempting to speculate that the de Roos shield was erected by Edmund during the few years when his authority was undisputed, 1485 to 1492. Edmund's sister, Eleanor de Roos, had married Sir Robert Manners, Sheriff of Northumberland, and their son, Sir George Manners, would eventually inherit the title Baron Roos in 1508. Thus, an alternative explanation for the shield may be that it was erected by Sir George Manners to mark his taking the title of 11th Baron Roos.

16th and 17th Centuries – Construction of the chancel clerestory and vestry. These changes arose out of the Reformation, with the adoption of St Mary's as a mausoleum by the Earls of Belvoir.

18th Century – little change except that the roofs reached their present form. E.A. Shipman stated that nave roof was not completed until 1740. It is plain, almost crude when compared with those in many other parish churches. Only in the transepts is there a greater degree of refinement, including a rose boss in the centre of the south transept roof.

Late 18th to 19th Century – St Mary's had become rather dilapidated by the late 18th Century. Restoration of the tombs was undertaken by curate William Mounsey in the 1780s, and they have been further repaired since. In 1847, under the leadership of Canon Frederick Norman, bench pews were installed by Messrs Broadbent & Hawley of Leicester. The choir loft was removed and an organ added by 1859. The tower was renovated by Sir Gilbert Scott who, in the 1860s, corrected a dangerous tilt that had developed. New stained-glass memorial windows were installed towards the end of the 19th Century, but there was also removal of medieval stained glass from the clerestory, a

At the third springer the south aisle arcade, a distorted face.

fraction of which was recovered and placed in the westernmost window of the chancel clerestory where it is seen today.

Remains of the medieval Doom painting were assessed in 1967 by Eve Baker and Douglas Betts during restoration of the roof: their report being reproduced by E.A. Shipman in 1995. Though in poor condition, it is perhaps fortunate to have been spared during the removal of plaster during the 19th Century restoration.

We tentatively conclude that the Medieval carvings on the south aisle may belong to the first half of the 14th Century. Carvings on the north aisle are probably late 14th Century, those on the tower early 15th Century, those on the clerestory and south transept probably mid-15th Century, and those on the nave arcades mid to late 15th or even early 16th Century. Together these are a display of Late-Medieval art, to which we can add the Doom, the remains of medieval stained glass and also the Coddyngton and Freeman brasses in the chancel floor. They are what is left to us of the decorative richness of the pre-Reformation St. Mary's.

The tombs in the chancel are in marked contrast. They are essentially commemorative rather than devotional, realistic rather than allegorical, not essential to the liturgical purposes of the church. Nevertheless, they are sumptuous, exquisite and fascinating, marking the turbulent politics of the 16th and 17th Centuries. The Victorian stained glass marks the great period of church restoration of the 19th Century.

On the transverse arch of the south transept, a grimacing man wearing a collar and bridle.

Also in the north aisle, on the transverse arch at its eastern end are these faces, one plump with perhaps stumpy horns, the other perhaps a lion, sticking out its tongue.

Exterior of the Aisles

Gargoyles are mounted on the parapet of the wall of the south aisle and south porch. There is a tiny carved head located at one of the label-stops of the Decorated window between the porch and south transept. The other side of the hood of this window abuts against the stonework of the south transept, which was rebuilt in the 15th Century.

There are three gargoyles, carved as human and grotesque animal faces in a style that is distinct from the gargoyles on the tower (early 15th Century) and the south transept (mid 15th Century).

Carved face on the south aisle window.

The outside of the north aisle is different. Here there are carved faces at the ends of the hood moulds of the windows and the north door. There are also faces of unconfirmed age at the ends of the hood mould of the north transept window, and others on the capping of the buttresses supporting the corners of this transept. These are all beautifully done, realistic and emotionally expressive, full of character. Other faces are seen on the hood moulds of the gothic windows of the vestry, but these are simpler, like the windows themselves. The square-framed 'Tudor' windows of the vestry do not have carvings.

A gargoyle on the 14th Century porch. Rainwater stills drains through them, but nowadays channelled through more modern piping.

On the western gable of the north aisle, this face of terror is almost hidden behind the encroaching buttress of the tower.

A serene face, on the doorway in the north aisle.

Two faces on windows of the north aisle.

Heads on the ends of the cappings of the buttresses supporting the north transept.

Two heads, probably both of men despite the long hair (perhaps a 17th Century hair style), at the ends of the hood mould of the north transept window, but seeming to be stuck on rather than an integral part of the structure, and thus later than the Perpendicular window itself.

The Tower

The frieze which runs around all four sides of the tower, at the base of the parapet, displays a mixture of distorted, cartoon-like faces and fleurons (stylised flowers). The faces include mouth-pullers, cats or lions, and examples of a lady whose face is framed by a square head-dress (whose significance for the age of the tower is discussed below). The fleurons are of mixed designs, including one which is in fact a 'green man' with leaves emerging from his mouth. The frieze is also punctuated by gargoyles, two on each side, carved as human and animal forms including face-pullers and a bear wearing a bridle. Label stops of the windows immediately beneath the frieze are carved with more lifelike faces, one apparently of a prince, another a lady in a square head -dress.

These carvings, and hence the tower itself, have been considered to date from the early part of the 15th Century. The fleurons are reminiscent of those on the frieze of the Perpendicular Corpus Christi Chapel at St Wulfram's, Grantham, which has been dated to the period 1400-1440 by Philip Dixon (in *The Making of Grantham*). St Wulfram's is most notable for its Decorated architecture, including vividly carved figures and large numbers of ball-flowers. The contrast between Decorated and Perpendicular carvings there supports the conclusion that the carvings at Bottesford tower, and the tower itself, are of the early 15th Century.

There are about a dozen examples of women's heads framed by a square head-dress at St Mary's. Lionel Wall has discussed their wider occurrence and proposed (*personal communication*) that they belong within an end-14th to early 15th Century period, on the basis of comparison with trends in contemporary late medieval head-dresses fashions.

Looking up at the tower and spire of St Mary's.

Three gargoyles on the tower, with mouths for water spouts (behind each is an opening of the rainwater gutters): left - on the south side of the tower, a cat-like creature ; centre - again on the southern side, a man's head clasped between his hands; right - on the northern side, a lion displaying his teeth.

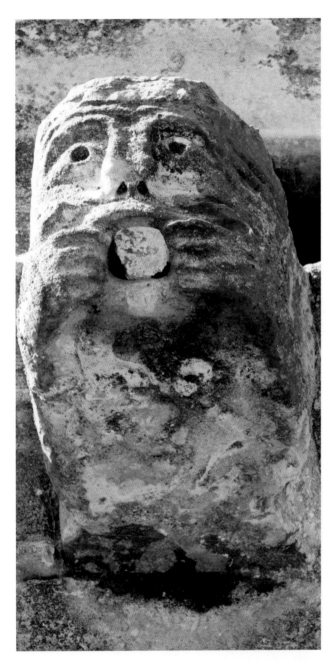  

Three more gargoyles: left - on the eastern side of the tower, a man holding his mouth agape; centre - west side of the tower, a woman in a square head -dress holding her mouth stretched open; right - east side of the tower, a bear in a bridle.

Six of the small grotesque faces carved in the stones forming the frieze below the parapet of the tower.

25

Carvings of flowers (fleurons) and one of a green man on the tower parapet frieze. Though there is variety in the floral designs, there are none of the ballflower design characteristic of early 14th Century friezes.

The southern aspect of the nave, showing the porch and south transept, above them the unbroken row of windows of the clerestory with their carved figures, some almost hidden from view by the transept. One might wonder why they were put there.

Gargoyles on the south transept - The "bellman" or "tollman".

The western of the gargoyles on the parapet of the south transept. This almost life-size figure was carved in great detail, with clappers in his bells and buttons on his coat. His robust, jovial appearance suggests perhaps an invitation to the market rather than a religious intent.

A boy's face on the window of the south transept.

Gargoyles on the south transept - The "alewife"

The eastern gargoyle: again, there is considerable detail, despite the centuries of exposure to the elements. She has a bowl in one hand, a jug in the other. Dating from the 15th Century, she may be announcing the church-ale.

A benign face on the window of the south transept.

Exterior of the Clerestory

The clerestory appears to have been constructed later than the tower, perhaps around the middle of the 15th Century, ostensibly to let more light into the nave. It comprises two east-west walls topped by parapets and pinnacles built above the nave arcades. The clerestory windows form close-spaced series in both these walls, eleven on either side, grouped into five pairs, corresponding precisely with the arcade arches beneath them, and an odd one at the eastern end to accommodate the greater width of the transept arches. Each pair shares a single internal mullion, but between the pairs the mullions are separated, allowing space for a slender column of masonry which carries the external down-pipe. On the inside, these broader spaces are used as the locations for the corbels that support the low-pitched wooden roof.

Both the north and south walls carry internal and external arrays of figurative carvings. The externals ones, both north and south, share a style and content that set them apart from the internal carvings. These latter, again both north and south, comprise two sets of carvings, one consisting of demons, wise men, angels and strange carvings rather like bouquets of flowers, located at the springers within the pairs of window arches, the other being the roof corbels located between the pairs of windows and carved as angels holding banners and shields. It seems likely that three different masons or sets of masons were at work here. Together, they created work of high quality.

Looking first at the external clerestory carvings, it quickly becomes clear that from the ground you can't in fact see them properly. They are hidden by the

The head of a bearded prophet on the southern side of the clerestory.

aisles unless you stand back at a distance, and even then the transepts conceal some almost completely. On both the northern and southern elevations there are essentially two rows, one above the other. The lower

On the south clerestory, one of two dragons that gaze down as though in anticipation of rich pickings among the sinners below.

consists of figures located at the springers of the window arches, both within and between each pair of windows. The upper row consists of gargoyle figures set in the base of the parapets between the pairs of windows where down-pipes emerged. In fact, none of the rows are complete, either because figures have fallen (or been removed) or were never put there in the first place. Nevertheless, there are more figures in the lower rows than in the upper, and it is in the lower rows that the best work is seen. Both rows are carried on to the eastern corners of the clerestory walls, where additional figures are located.

The overall scheme of carvings is shown in the table below, in which their positions are numbered sequentially from the eastern end of the clerestory. The intention is to see if there is any correlation between the carvings on either side of the clerestory. However, it is apparent from this table that there are both differences and correspondences between the schemes on the northern and southern sides. On the northern side is a queen, three examples of carvings in which a man is accompanied by a dragon, and three semi-human figures referred to here as the 'pig-like man', the 'bird-man' and the 'scaly devil-man': none of these are seen on the southern side, which is distinct in having a prince, a prophet, a priest, a man raising his hands, and a bear wearing a bridle.

A table comparing the positions of the grotesques on the clerestories on either side of the nave.

Position	North side lower row	North side upper row	South side lower row	South side upper row
Eastern corner	dragon	paired man and dragon	man in head covering	winged bird-man
1	pig-like man	nothing	man in head covering	nothing
2	paired man and dragon	scaly devil-man	broken dragon	bear in bridle
3	dragon	nothing	man holding hands up	nothing
4	broken	nothing	priest	lutanist
5	dragon	nothing	dragon	nothing
6	paired man and dragon	bird-man	broken figure	broken
7	**king**	nothing	**king**	nothing
8	non-figurative	nothing	non-figurative	nothing
9	**queen**	nothing	**prince**	nothing
10	piper	harpist	dragon	broken
11	dragon	nothing	prophet	nothing
12	dragon	nothing	dragon	nothing

A dragon carving on the northern side of the clerestory.

What the two sides have in common are a king (at the same position on both sides), musicians (a piper and a harpist to the north, a lutanist on the southern side) and several winged dragons. The north-side king has a long thin face with a forked beard and bushy moustache, a sword in his right hand, a possible mace in his left, a crown on his head. His southern counterpart has an orb in his left hand, a sword (lost) in his right, and a crown on his head. They are not copies, and may represent particular monarchs. The queen holds a censor in her right hand, a mace in her left, a crown on her head, her long hair merging with the carved foliage. The prince is clean-shaven and fresh-faced, crowned, holding a large book (probably the Bible) open in his hands. Again, he seems to represent a particular person, but who this might be is conjectural. All these carvings are of high quality, many in good condition despite their years. The head of the prophet is especially attractive. Many are carvings worked in single blocks of stone that are structurally part of the window arches. Two of the dragons on the southern side appear to have been put in place slightly later, but all the others are integral to the structure, as are the figures of ordinary people, such as the musicians, the priest, the man in a close-fitting costume with rows of buttons (is he a jester?) holding up his hands, fingers stretched, as though imploring someone to go no further. Some of the figures jutting out from the parapet appear to depict dual human-animals, as if showing a man as we see him alongside his true base nature.

On the southern side of the clerestory, a prince and a king. Their identities are not recorded.

33

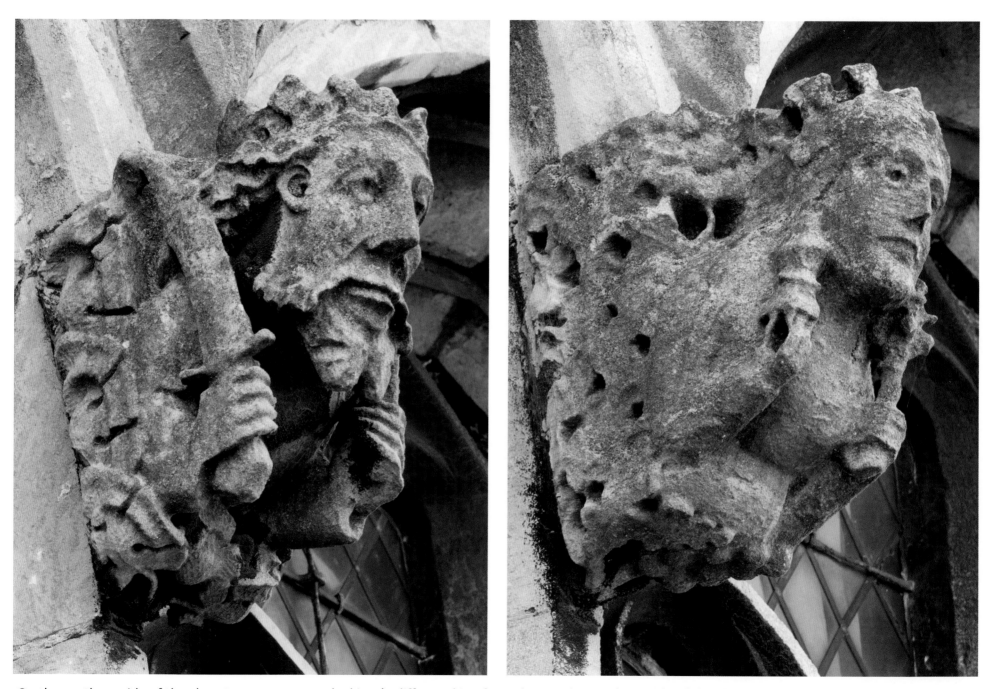

On the northern side of the clerestory, a queen and a king (a different king from that on the southern side of the clerestory, depicted in the preceding page).

On the south clerestory, a winged dragon, and a hooded man, perhaps a fool or a jester, holding up his hands as though giving a warning.

A bagpiper, on the northern side of the clerestory.

A double carving, showing a bearded man with his arm around a pig-like demonic figure, perhaps his alter-ego, on the northern side of the clerestory .

Two figures located on the eastern corner of the southern side of the clerestory. The lower one is a bearded man wearing a cloth head-dress. This is not a king, but his dignified, bearded face and garments suggest a prominent person, perhaps a judge or a nobleman. The upper is a winged creature with scaly legs ending in paws or clawed feet, and a human face.

Two views of the upper carving at the eastern end of the northern side of the clerestory, depicting the double figure of a man, apparently holding a sword in his right hand and a small, circular shield or drum in his left, accompanied by a winged dragon-like creature bearing its fearsome teeth.

The man, with a strangely bulbous chin, looks anxious, but the dragon appears to be smiling. In Medieval theology the Devil was likened to a dragon because he was the worst of all serpents. This carving can be interpreted as showing a sinner who seems to have been ensnared by the Dragon/Devil.

A figure with dragon's wings, folded human-like legs and a dog-like face, the lower carving on the eastern end of the northern side of the clerestory.

St Mary's church and graveyard, seen from the northeast.

Interior of the Clerestory

On the inside of the clerestory, roof corbels carved as angels are mounted on the slender columns of stones that separate the pairs of windows. These are rather static in appearance, the angels wearing head-bands adorned with simple crosses stand on carved plinths which form the bases of the corbels. Some have blackened eye pupils. Half of them hold shields, the others hold ribbon-like banners, and these two types alternate along the rows of corbels and also across the clerestory, so that each angel holding a shield on one side faces an angel holding a banner on the opposite side. However, each corbel angel is distinctive in its facial features, head-dress, clothing and plinth. Their shields and banners would once have been adorned with lettering or heraldic symbols, but none of these remain.

The inside of the clerestory: light is flooding in, but it may be hard to see the carvings.

The angel-corbels alternate with carvings located at the internal springers within each pair of windows. On the northern side of the clerestory there are five, which comprise three truly demonic faces, gazing over the congregation below, and two odd sculptures interpreted as sheaves of flowers of some description. The demonic figures have blackened pupils, making them appear doubly sinister. This appears to be part of their original decoration. Many of the other carved figures have hollow pupils to their eyes, and it may be that some at least of these were originally filled with lead. Lionel Wall (*personal communication*) describes this in his work on church carvings in southeast Leicestershire, noting that plugs of black lead were used in some instances.

On the southern side of the clerestory, in marked contrast, the alternating carvings comprise two heads of what may be wise men or prophets (or kings), and three carvings of angels, two carrying shields and the other carrying a ribbon-like banner. This appears to be the 'good' side, in contrast with the demonic figures opposite ("the Devil's Shadow"). The wise faces may represent specific figures, but just who they might be is uncertain.

The roof of the nave is supported by stone corbels carved as angels, some holding scrolls, others holding shields. As with many of the other carvings mounted close beneath the roof, these have their eyes picked out in black paint, in these cases applied to the pupils rather than the whole eyes as in the case of the demonic carvings.

43

Previous page - Some of the most striking and perhaps unexpected carvings are between the windows of the clerestory, high up near the roof. There is little light, so that these are difficult to see (and not so easy to photograph), yet they are expertly and extravagantly carved blocks of limestone. Muzzles glare down with tongues lolling. Eyes are blackened, in contrast to the otherwise bare stone, adding to their theatrically sinister appearance. One has wrinkled or corrugated skin and bat-like ears: the other has smoother skin and pronounced nostrils. Its tongue is extraordinary, sticking out and curling, yet apparently all part of the single carved block of stone. On the crown of the head is a strange crest, reminiscent of a tiara.

This head of an ape with long tresses, blackened malevolent eyes a toothless mouth and cleft palate. Attached to the lower lip is a disc-like object of uncertain significance.

A carving of a sheaf of flowers in the north clerestory interior.

Above the southern side of the nave are the heads of two bearded men. One appears to be a prophet (left), the other may be a king wearing a cap rather than a crown, with an oval jewel or badge attached at the front. In neither are the eyes painted black, though it appears that the pupils have been carved so that they stand out (or are they scooped back?) and may have black highlights positioned to create the appearance of a gaze directed upwards.

These carvings on the southern side of the clerestory are of angels, which seem to be almost floating above the nave. They carry a scroll-like banner or a shield, which would once have been painted, the scroll perhaps with music, the shield with a coat of arms.

Carvings in the Nave, a 'Sermon in Stone'

Unlike the carvings in the clerestory, those mounted at the springers of the arches of the nave are hard to miss. Near the eastern end of the arcades are the heraldic shields of Bishop John Marshall, who died in 1495, and facing it, on the northern side, that of the de Roos surmounted by the peacock emblem of de Roos (later adopted by the Earls of Rutland). Right at the eastern end are a woman (or a priest?) to the south and a king on the northern side, gazing at each other while their bodies seem to be sliding down the stonework.

The other figures in the nave are all of monstrous creatures. Although today we might look at these as works of art in their own right, this was not the objective of their creators. They were there to provide moral guidance for medieval viewers. They are literally "sermons in stone" intended to demonstrate the belief that the world itself was the Word of God, and that every living thing has its own special meaning within Creation, a book of nature designed by God as a source of instruction for humanity. This idea was partly based upon biblical studies but mostly upon one of the most popular of medieval books, the *Bestiary* or *Bestiarum Vocabulum.*

This two-headed 'amphisbaena', spits and snarls from between the 2nd and 3rd arches of the north arcade.

An Amphisbaena, from the 13th century bestiary text "Summa de vitiis" in the British Library, Harley MS3244 Folio 62.

47

The head of a woman (or is it a monk?), on the eastern pilaster of the southern arcade.

The image of John Marshall, Bishop of Llandaff, which stands on top of the carving of his shield above the first pillar of the south nave arcade.

The head of a king, on the eastern pilaster of the northern arcade.

Mounted above the first pillar of the north nave arcade, a shield bearing the de Roos arms, surmounted by a helmet (or a Cap of Maintenance) and the Peacock resplendent, the emblem of both the de Roos and Manners families.

This animal, on the north arcade of the nave, may be a wolf, a she-wolf or perhaps a hyena. All represent forms of evil.

The Biblical text which was most important as an inspiration for medieval sculpture was taken from the Book of Job which in the King James Bible says:-

But ask now the beasts, and they shall teach thee; and the fowls of the air, and they shall tell thee: Or speak to the earth, and it shall teach thee: and the fishes of the sea shall declare unto thee. Who knoweth not in all these that the hand of the Lord hath wrought this? Job (12:7-10)

Within the medieval mind the interpretation of this text, that God's design of the universe can provide literal moral guidance, was reinforced by the studies of the ancient Greek *Physiologus*, a 2nd Century Alexandrian text which summarized Aristotle's *Historia Animalium* and other classical authors. David Badkeon in his definitive website *The Medieval Bestiary* (*http://bestiary.ca/index.html*) writes:-

"The bestiary, or "book of beasts", is more than just an expansion of the Physiologus, though the two have much in common. The bestiary also describes a beast and uses that description as a basis for an allegorical teaching, but by including text from other sources it goes further; and while still not a "zoology textbook", it is not only a religious text, but also a description of the world as it was known.

The bestiary manuscripts were usually illustrated, sometimes lavishly, as for example in the Harley Bestiary and the Aberdeen Bestiary; the pictures served as a "visual language" for the illiterate public, who knew the stories - preachers used them in sermons - and would remember the moral teaching when they saw the beast depicted. Bestiary images could be found everywhere. They appeared not only in bestiaries but in manuscripts of all kinds; in churches and monasteries, carved in stone both inside and out, and in wood on misericords and on other decorated furniture; painted on walls and worked into mosaics; and woven into tapestries."

The Dragon and related mythical and actual animal carvings inside and outside of St Mary's can be seen as illustrations of the moral lessons of the Bestiary, but what then of the Angels? An explanation can be found in the writing of St.

We believe this to be an ape, representing deceit, an evil creature seen at the western end of the north nave arcade.

We believe this to be a lion, with its tongue sticking out, a virtuous creature seen at the western end of the south arcade.

Bernard of Clairvaux, the 12th century monk who was a major reformer of the Cistercian order. St Bernard seems, perhaps, to have anticipated some of what was later to become the Reformation Protestant suspicion of religious imagery, in 1127, when he wrote in criticism of bestiary type carvings :-

"What profit is there in those ridiculous monsters, in that marvellous and deformed comeliness, that comely deformity? To what purpose are those unclean apes, those fierce lions, those monstrous centaurs, those half men, those striped tigers, those fighting knights, those hunters winding their horns? Many bodies are seen under one head, or again many heads to one body. Here is a four-footed beast with a serpent's tail; there a fish with a beast's head. Here again the fore-part of a horse trails half a goat behind it, or a horned beast bears the hind quarters of a horse. In short, so many and marvellous are the varieties of shapes on every hand that we are tempted to read in the marble than in our books, and to spend the whole day wondering at these things rather than meditating the law of God. For God's sake, if men are not ashamed of these follies, why at least do they not shrink from the expense?"

One hypothesis which would explain the presence of such a wide variety of creatures in church carvings is that in the medieval period (indeed right up to the 18th century) *the description of the world as it was known* was that nature was organised according to a system known as The Great Chain of Being. Whereas we have an evolutionary model of natural history (that life began with simple animals which gradually evolved into more complex forms) they had a devolutionary model which argued that descending down from God through the Stars and Planets, and into and through mankind to the animals was a great system, the Great Chain, which linked all Creation in a harmonious unity.

One of the organizing principles of The Great Chain of Being was the Principle of Plenitude, which argued that every single link in the chain had to be filled for the system to function. For many Medieval thinkers there were gaps in the devolutionary chain, as for example between Men and Apes, which were too large for the Principle of Plenitude to work properly.

Mythical man-like creatures, including a Cyclops (bottom let). Copyright of the Dean and Chapter of Westminster, reproduced by kind permission.

They sought intermediate 'missing links', men or animals, to fill in those spaces. These were St Bernard's *"monstrous centaurs, those half men, Many bodies are seen under one head, or again many heads to one body. Here is a four-footed beast with a serpent's tail; there a fish with a beast's head. Here again the fore-part of a horse trails half a goat behind it, or a horned beast bears the hind quarters of a horse."* Many bestiary books have pages of illustrations of intermediate people perhaps for this reason. Some of the carvings at St Mary's seem to have been designed to illustrate the system of descent through the Great Chain, including intermediate or composite figures and animals. An example is the carving of a single eyed Cyclops-style face from just below the chancel arch of St Mary's. This can be compared with an illustration from the c.13th century Westminster Abbey Bestiary, which shows a similar Cyclops figure on the bottom left, along with many other variations on the human form. Other examples are the carving of double figures, perhaps depicting the good and evil sides of human nature, on the north outer clerestory.

An illustration of the Great Chain of Being, from Llull (1304, published 1512).

52

A Manticore gapes and snarls from between the 3rd and 4th arches of the north arcade. David Badkeon describes it thus:- *"The Manticore is a composite beast from India, with a lion's body, the face of a man with blue eyes, and a tail resembling the sting of a scorpion. It can leap great distances and is very active. It eats human flesh. Its voice is a whistle that sounds like a melody from pipes. Some say it can shoot spines from its tail."* The illustration, from a Bestiary called the *Summa de vitiis* which dates from the 2nd or 3rd quarter of the 13th century, and is in the British Library, shows a naked man being mauled by a Manticore. The tail of our St Mary's Manticore has perhaps been damaged and may once have shown the full scorpion style stinger.

In contrast to the Manticore, the Lion was seen as a benevolent creature. Lions were frequently carved with their tongues out in a licking posture, as in the two examples from the south nave arcade and the northern springer of

The 'manticore', an evil creature with the body of a lion and head of a man, though with sharp fangs, gapes and snarls from the northern nave arcade.

A manticore devouring its victim. British Library, Harley 3244 Folio 43v

the Chancel arch. The illustration from an early 12th century Bestiary perhaps explains why, as it says in the British Library caption for the illustration:- " *Two adult lions lick their cubs. The lioness gives birth to dead cubs, which remain inanimate until their father arrives after three days and breathes in their faces. Many characteristics of lions link them allegorically to Christ, and this particular trait symbolises Christ's resurrection on his third day in the tomb. The image of the lions licking rather than breathing upon their cubs may draw upon Pliny's 'Historia naturalis', which states that lions' cubs are born unformed and must be licked into shape.*"

The carving on the south arcade of a rather mournful-looking lion.

Lions licking their new-born cubs into life. British Library Royal MS12CXIX Folio 6

Looking eastwards through the chancel arch into the chancel itself, with its tombs and the east window.

The blind doorway that once gave access to the rood loft.

The faces of a cyclops and a lion, between the rood loft door and the chancel arch. The lion's tongue is sticking out, suggesting a link to the lion carvings in the nave (p.54).

Trumpeters and saints at the Day of Judgement

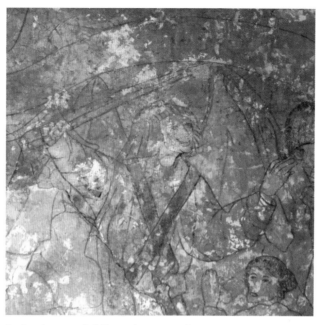

St Andrew wielding the sword.

A repentant sinner before the mouth of Hell

The dead reborn, rising from their graves

The 'Doom' painting

Removal of plaster from the chancel arch revealed traces of a Doom painting. The central part, with Christ enthroned, has been lost, but a large part of the lateral parts were uncovered, though in poor condition. It was examined in 1967 by Mrs Eve Baker and Mr Douglas Betts who considered it to have been painted post-1450 and pre-1525. Angels sound the trumpets, resurrected souls rise from their graves, St Michael weighs souls, St Andrew wields the sword to keep the devil at bay. At the extreme right hand side demons goad condemned souls into the gaping Leviathan mouth of Hell.

A demon pushes sinners into Hell

Tombs and Monuments

The 1530s were a watershed in English history, when Henry VIII commanded the social and structural changes of the English Reformation. St Mary's started to be used as the mausoleum of the Earls and Dukes of Rutland and their families. However, the oldest of the tombs and effigies in the chancel are of members of the de Roos. This family held Belvoir Castle and its estates from 1247 until, after an interval spanning most of the Wars of the Roses and the reign of Henry VII, they passed, on the death of Edmund 10th Baron Roos in 1508, to Sir George Manners, son of Sir Robert Manners of Etal and his wife the co-heiress Eleanor de Roos.

Sir Robert de Roos, 1st Baron Roos, d.1285.

This Purbeck Marble effigy on the north wall of the Chancel was brought from Croxton Abbey during the Dissolution of the Monastries (1536-1541). It depicts a late 13th century knight wearing a hooded hauberk of chain mail under a loose sleeveless surcoat, mail gauntlets, a sword and belt on the left side together with a shield. It is accompanied by a plaque known as the 'Heart Stone', also from Croxton Abbey, whose inscription records the burial of the heart of Robert de Roos at Croxton. In translation, the inscription reads: 'Here lies the heart of Lord Robert de Roos, whose body is buried at Kirkham, who died on 13th May AD 1285. Isabella Lady de Roos, wife of the said Robert de Roos, was buried at New Place (Newstead) near Stamford, who died AD 1301". She was the last of the Albini line at Belvoir. Her intricately carved sandstone effigy can be seen in St Mary's, Orston, where it was moved to from Newstead (near Stamford).

One of the angel panels of the tomb of Sir John de Roos: there are traces of the original red paint on his left wing.

Sir William de Roos, 7th Baron Roos, d. 1414.

South of the altar is the alabaster tomb and effigy of William de Roos, a supporter of Henry Bolingbroke (Henry IV). This tomb together with that of his eldest son John (below) was brought from Belvoir Priory on the Dissolution of the Monasteries. The effigy and decorated base chest suggest the work of the Chellaston school of sculptors in Derbyshire. The armour is a mixture of mail and plate. A conical bascinet helmet with a jewelled margin is worn while under the head is a tilting-heaume and a peacock . On the front of the helmet is "IHC NASARE" (Jesus of Nazareth) and from the helmet hangs a tippet of chain mail over which is a decorative SS collar (SS stands for 'Souvenir Sovereign' - remember your king, a Lancastrian emblem). The insignia of the Garter is worn on the left leg. Behind the tomb is an Early English piscina.

Sir John de Roos, 8th Baron Roos, d.1421.

North of the altar is the alabaster tomb and effigy, brought from Belvoir Priory, of John, son of Sir William de Roos, who fought at Agincourt but lost his life at the decisive French victory at Baugé in 1421. Lord John also wears a conical bascinet with an orle, his head resting on a tilt-heaume which once bore the de Roos peacock crest. The alabaster is marked by graffiti, some of considerable age.

The descriptions of armour and costume draw on M.P. Dare's guide published in 1950.

Thomas Manners, 1st Earl of Rutland, 12th Baron de Roos (1492–1543) and Countess Eleanor (née Paston) (d.1551).

This is the first of the eight earls' tombs in St Mary's. Earl Thomas is depicted in mail and full plate armour, over which he wears the mantle of The Order of the Garter, while on his left leg is the Garter itself. The coronet is supported by the tilt-heaume complete with the "Cap of Maintenance" and peacock crest. Countess Eleanor Paston, his second wife, wears a gown, a short cape and an ermine-trimmed mantle fastened by a cordon, her feet on a griffon. The chest is decorated with pilasters, swags and "weepers" thought to be children of the family. The tomb was created by Richard Parker of Burton on Trent. The body was embalmed with spices from Nottingham and encased in wax. A plumber then encased it in a close fitting leaden shell. Masons had to strengthen the chancel floor to bear the weight before his extravagant funeral for which the black palls and hangings alone cost £160 (what would that be today?).

The 9th Baron Roos had been attainted by Edward IV in 1461 after the battle of Towton, and was finally captured and beheaded after the Battle of Hexham in 1464. Belvoir was granted to Sir William Hastings who held both the Castle and the manor of Bottesford for about twenty years during which the Castle was allowed to fall into ruins. However, Edmund, 10th Baron Roos, had the confiscation reversed and his lands returned In 1485. He died in 1508, childless. His sister, Eleanor, had married Sir Robert Manners, thus creating the present Manners line. Their grandson was Sir Thomas Manners, 12th Baron de Roos, who received the Order of the Garter and in April 1525 was created 1st Earl of Rutland by Henry VIII. He had been called to Parliament in 1515 and was present when Henry VIII met the French king Charles V at the Field of Cloth of Gold in 1520, then became cupbearer to the King in 1521. He was involved in

The alabaster effigy of Thomas, 1st Earl of Rutland.

The alabaster effigy of Countess Eleanor , wife of the 1st Earl of Rutland.

the hearings regarding the legality of Henry VIII's marriage to Katherine of Aragon. After initially displaying sympathy towards Katherine, he became a close supporter of Henry's actions. He helped Henry with the divorce and was one of the generals who suppressed the Catholic monastic rebellion of 1536 in Yorkshire and Lincolnshire, known as the Pilgrimage of Grace.

The 1st Earl of Rutland was present at Henry VIII's marriage to Anne Boleyn in 1533, then took part in her trial three years later. When Anne of Cleves came to England, Rutland was appointed her lord chamberlain. His second wife Eleanor Manners (née Paston, c.1495 - 1551) was lady-in-waiting successively to Anne Boleyn, Jane Seymour, Anne of Cleves and Catherine Howard. As senior lady-in-waiting to Anne of Cleves, she knew that the marriage was unconsummated. Anne reportedly praised Henry to her as a good husband saying, *"When he comes to bed he kisseth me, and he taketh me by the hand, and biddeth me 'Good night, sweetheart'; and in the morning kisseth me and biddeth 'Farewell, darling'."* Lady Rutland responded: *"Madam, there must be more than this, or it will be long ere we have a duke of York, which all this realm most desireth."*

In 1524, Thomas inherited Elsing Palace, Middlesex, from his great-uncle, Sir Thomas Lovell, and soon afterwards sold it to King Henry. He was then able to commence the re-building of Belvoir Castle. The re-building work was completed by his son, the 2nd Earl of Rutland. At the Dissolution of the Monasteries, Thomas was granted both Belvoir Priory and Croxton Abbey (and other monastic properties and lands), and he ensured that many of the monuments to his family were removed to St Mary's. He was patron of St. Mary's during the Henrician reforms and began the re-shaping of the chancel for its role as the mausoleum of the Earls of Rutland.

'Weepers' on the tomb chest of Earl Thomas and Countess Eleanor. They seem to represent their children, though M.P. Dare tells us that there are perhaps too many for this to be literally true. The panels retain traces of the paint they were originally covered with.

Henry Manners, 2nd Earl of Rutland (1543-1563) and Countess Margaret (née Neville), d.1560.

The earl wears armour, his head resting on a tilt-heaume. On his left leg is the Garter. He holds a sword in his left hand, a prayer book in his right. Countess Margaret, daughter of Ralph Neville, Earl of Westmorland, wears a coronet and an ermine-trimmed mantle, her head on a scroll. On the overlying table are the figures of their children. Following the death of Countess Margaret, the Earl married Bridget, daughter of Lord Hussey of Sleaford, who lived until 1600.

During the twenty years of Henry Manners' earldom England had four monarchs, Henry VIII and his three children, Edward VI (1547-53), Mary I (1553-58) and Elizabeth I (1558-1603), each of whom followed a different strand of religious belief. Edward, a strict Protestant, supported the destruction of religious images and transformation of churches into white spaces decorated only with biblical texts. Mary, a devout Catholic, strove to restore the Catholic church and suppress the Protestants. Elizabeth I, the last of the Tudors, created a church which was Protestant but followed some Catholic forms and ceremonies, a compromise called the Elizabethan Settlement. A major point of dispute was the form of the rite of communion, either kneeling at the altar in the Catholic manner or sitting at a table in the nave in the way of the Calvinists. The Earl and his Lady show their confusion at all this religious change and lie not on the traditional altar tomb but underneath a Protestant altar table. He is holding The Book of Common Prayer, whereas she appears to hold a different prayer book, possibly an older Book of Hours reflecting her catholic faith.

During the reign of Edward VI, Henry Manners supported the reformed Protestant party in church matters and was close to John Dudley, the Lord Protector, who led the government of the young King from 1550 until 1553, and unsuccessfully tried to install Lady Jane Grey as Queen after Edward VI's death. The Earl of Rutland was appointed Warden of

Tomb of Henry, 2nd Earl of Rutland, and Countess Margaret .

The magnificent alabaster effigies of the Henry, 2nd Earl of Rutland, and Countess Margaret, lying side by side.

the Scottish Marches in 1549, and then Lord Lieutenant of Nottinghamshire in 1552. On Mary's accession in 1553 he was imprisoned as a supporter of Lady Jane Grey, but came to terms with Mary's Government after Lady Jane Grey's and Northampton's executions. He was made an admiral and took part in the Italian War of 1551-1559, serving as Captain-General of the cavalry in the English victory at St Quentin in 1557. Continued fighting during 1558 resulted in the loss of Calais, England's last stronghold in France (a defeat said to have broken Queen Mary's heart!). After these events, the earl was placed in command of the defence of Dover against possible French invasion. He subsequently became a favourite of Elizabeth I, who in 1559 made him a Knight of the Garter and Lord Lieutenant of Rutland. He was made Lord President of the North and in 1561 an ecclesiastical commissioner for the reforms of the Church of England that resulted in the Act of Settlement. He died in 1563, not long after completing the re-building of Belvoir Castle.

Elizabeth, daughter of the 3rd Earl and Countess, kneels at the foot of her parent's tomb.

Edward Manners, 3rd Earl of Rutland (1563-1587) and Countess Isabel (née Holcroft).

The alabaster tomb, by the Flemish craftsman Gerard Johanssen (Johnson) of Southwark, is the first of the four richly canopied examples in the Church. These are complex and intricately carved constructions of alabaster, vividly painted to make the figures almost life-like. Earl Edward is shown in full plate armour, wearing the mantle of the Order of the Garter with the Garter itself on his left leg. Countess Isabel, daughter of Sir Thomas Holcroft, wears a ruff with the usual dress of the time under an ermine trimmed mantle. A rich cushion supports her head. Their only daughter, Elizabeth, kneels at her feet.

Born in 1549, Edward Manners, eldest son of the 2nd Earl of Rutland, inherited the title in 1563 at the age of 14. He was made a ward of the Queen Elizabeth, and placed under the charge of Sir William Cecil, 1st Baron Burghley. This relationship led to all of his offices of state. The first was when, aged 20, he served as a commander of Queen Elizabeth's forces against the northern earls who had rebelled in support of Mary Queen of Scots and her possible marriage with the catholic Duke of Norfolk. Edward became a Lieutenant and Colonel of Foot in the forces led by the Earl of Sussex. In the event the rebellion petered out and Mary Queen of Scots went into the long period of arrest and confinement which was only ended by her execution in 1586. Edward Manners also played a role in that drama, in that he was one of the commissioners who tried and condemned the Scottish Queen following the Babington plot, a government trap engineered by William Cecil and Francis Walsingham. Edward married Isabel, daughter of Sir Thomas Holcroft. Their daughter Elizabeth was married at the age of 13 to the grandson of William Cecil. Tragically, she never fully recovered from childbirth at the age of 14 and died aged 15 in London. She is commemorated as the kneeling figure at the foot of the tomb. Her father served as England's Lord Chancellor for just two days in 1587 before his death at the age of 38. The Earl died on Good Friday, 14th April 1587, at Puddle Wharf, London, and was brought home for burial on 11th May.

The effigies of Edward Manners, 3rd Earl of Rutland (d.1587), and Countess Isabel lying side by side on their tomb.

John Manners, 4th Earl of Rutland (1587-1588), and Countess Elizabeth (née Charlton), d.1613.

Opposite the tomb of his elder brother, Edward, is that of John the 4th Earl (born 1552) and Countess Elizabeth. Gerard Johanssen again was the sculptor, both tombs being created at the same time, in 1591. John lived only ten months after Edward's death and died on 24th February 1588 at Nottingham. Countess Elizabeth, daughter of Francis Charlton, then had the dubious pleasure of ordering both the 3rd Earl's as well as her husband's monuments. There were nine children , of whom two died in infancy.

John became the 4th Earl of Rutland in year of the Great Armada, 1588. Although he had a military career in the Irish wars, John Manners is now chiefly remembered as the father of a large family. No less than three of his sons, Roger, Francis, and George, became Earls of Rutland. Oliver, the fifth son, was suspected of involvement in the Gunpowder Plot having been converted to Catholicism by the Jesuit John Gerard, a close friend of the Plot leader Robert Catesby. He was serving as MP for Grantham in November 1605 but failed to warn the authorities about the conspiracy. He went into exile in 1606, was ordained to the Jesuit priesthood at Rome in 1611, and returned to England before dying in London in 1613.

Countess Elizabeth became the *de-facto* Earl during the minority of her eldest surviving son Roger and proved to be a formidable administrator, founding the Countess of Rutland's Hospital in Bottesford, amongst many other things. She arranged her sons Roger and Francis' educational visits to Europe, outlined on their tombs in the church, which were something of a prototype for the 18th century Grand Tour.

Effigy of John, the 4th Earl, and Countess Elizabeth, with their youngest daughter, Elizabeth, at their head.

Three sons of the 4th Earl of Rutland, weepers on their parent's tomb, from left to right: Roger (later the 5th Earl), Francis (later the 6th Earl) and George (later the 7th Earl).

Effigies of four more of the surviving children of the 4th Earl of Rutland and Countess Elizabeth. We tentatively identify them, from the left, as Frances, Oliver, Bridget and Edward (who died as an infant). One more of the daughters is missing from the tomb altogether.

The heraldic lion, crouching at the foot of Countess Elizabeth.

Roger Manners, 5th Earl of Rutland (1588–1612) and Countess Elizabeth (née Sidney), 1585-1612.

Next to the altar rail on the north side of the chancel is the tomb of Earl Roger and his Countess Elizabeth, in alabaster, the work of Nicholas, son of Gerard Johanssen. It cost £150 including carriage by sea from London to Boston. Earl Roger is in half armour and an ermine-trimmed mantle with a tippet and wears a coronet. A cushion supports his head and a peacock is at his feet. Elizabeth wears a close fitting cap, coronet, ruff and bodiced gown under her ermine trimmed mantle and tippet. A richly embroidered cushion supports her head.

Roger Manners had been one of Queen Elizabeth's wards following the death of his father in 1588, and was placed under Sir William Cecil, together with Robert Devereux, 2nd Earl of Essex. However his relationship with the Cecils was anything but close. Seemingly influenced by Essex, he came to regard Cecil's hard-headed statecraft irredeemably vulgar, and they sought a more courtly way of conducting affairs of state. Roger Manners travelled widely on the continent between 1595-98, then in 1599 became a Colonel of the Infantry in the force Essex led to fight the rebellion of the Earl of Tyrone. The Queen forbade the earl from going, fearing Essex's increasing power, but in April he slipped out of England and in May was knighted by Essex before being summoned back for disobeying the Queen's orders. Essex, realising that the campaign was a fiasco, concluded a private truce with Tyrone, to the Queen's' fury. He rode back overnight and famously burst into the Queen's apartments in an attempt to explain his agreement. She was angry and probably frightened of the possibility of assassination and a coup. Essex was placed under house arrest, but on February 8th 1601, with Roger Manners as his third of command, he led a group of nobles and gentlemen (some later involved in the Gunpowder Plot) to raise a rebellion. They expected to receive popular support, but none was forthcoming. Essex was found guilty of treason and beheaded. Rutland was imprisoned in the Tower and fined £30,000, a huge

A cherubic face on the tomb of the 5th Earl and Countess Elizabeth.

amount, but was fortunate not to have lost his life.

In 1599, he had married Elizabeth Sidney, daughter of Sir Phillip Sidney, the poet, military hero and role model for Elizabethan men of letters, who had died heroically fighting the Spanish in 1586. Sir Philip Sydney's funeral was a major state event, gaining him the status of a Protestant martyr. Countess Elizabeth was also the grand-daughter of Sir Francis Walsingham, Queen Elizabeth's master spy, and as the result of her mother's re-marriage she was step-daughter of the ill-fated Earl of Essex. She was said to have been dismayed by her exile from court life following her husband's punishment.

The effigies of Roger Manners, 5th Earl of Rutland, who died in 1612, and Countess Elizabeth, who died in the same year.

Ben Jonson wrote the first of three poems to her in 1600, *The Epistle to the Countess of Rutland*, in which he tactfully withdrew a verse about the imminent birth of a son on hearing that the Earl was in fact impotent.

James VI of Scotland was proclaimed James I of England in 1603, and crossed into England on April 6th. Because of plague in London, he made a slow journey south, and on April 10th reached Belvoir Castle, where he stayed for two weeks. He had been receiving an annuity of £4000 from Queen Elizabeth, under the settlement negotiated by the 3rd Earl, and this probably helped restoration of Earl Roger's political fortunes. The Earl was appointed ambassador to Denmark, with orders to invest King Christian IV with the Order of the Garter and to convey gifts on the christening of his first son, an important role because of the close links between the Danish and Scottish thrones. Roger Manners evidently enjoyed his visit to the Danish court. The accountant John Brewer, who accompanied him, records what was almost a royal progress of the Earl's party to Copenhagen and Elsinore, with lavish spending on food, entertainment, and munificent gifts to the poor. The fact that *Hamlet* was altered to improve the description of Elsinore in the 1605 edition, published shortly after the Rutland visit, has led some scholars to claim that Roger Manners actually *was* Shakespeare! Indeed, Ilya Gililov has argued that both Roger and Elizabeth Manners were the true authors of Shakespeare's work. However this is very much a fringe opinion, rejected by mainstream of Shakespeare scholarship.

Countess Elizabeth gathered poets and admirers around her, including Ben Jonson, the playwright Francis Beaumont who worked for Shakespeare's King's Men, and Sir Thomas Overbury who was murdered in one of the most notorious of Jacobean conspiracies. She danced in the *Masque of Hymenaei*, a spectacular entertainment written by Jonson and designed by Inigo Jones, staged in Whitehall in 1606 to celebrate the marriage of her step-brother Robert Devereux, 3rd Earl of Essex, to Frances Howard, daughter of the Earl of Suffolk, a marriage designed by King James and Robert Cecil to reconcile the factions divided by the Essex rebellion.

The 5th Earl died childless on 26th June 1612 at Cambridge. At his funeral there were: 203 Retainers and Servants, 9 Clergy and 27 Cooks. Costs included £145 Herald's fees, £5 Black draperies, £30 Doles for the poor, £20 Southwell Minster Choir, £20 Embalming fee, 16s. for 16 men ringing at the Funeral, 6 mourning gowns given to the people of Bottesford. Elizabeth died in August 1612, two months after Roger Manners' death. A contemporary, John Chamberlain, reported a family rumour that she was poisoned by Sir Walter Raleigh, and her death was the subject of an extremely angry poem by Beaumont, *An Elegy on the Death of the Virtuous Lady Elizabeth Countess of Rutland*. According to Chamberlain, she had been planning to marry a member of the Howard faction with what was considered indecent haste. Ben Jonson said of her that she was as talented a poet as her father. However, none of her poems have been uncovered to date.

The winged skull and hourglass mounted on the top of the tomb of he 5th Earl and Countess: memento mori, a reminder that we all must die.

Francis Manners, 6th Earl of Rutland (1612–1632), Countesses Frances (née Knyvet), d.1608, and Countess Cecilia (née Tufton), d.1653.

Southwest of the altar is the massive tomb of Earl Francis, born in 1578, third son of the 4th Earl and Countess Elizabeth. Its height required the roof of the chancel to be raised and even then the peacock crest was only accommodated by cutting away part of a rafter. The Earl lies below Countess Frances, his first wife, and above Countess Cecilia, his second. He is shown entirely in court dress, with the Garter and the mantle of the Order, a sword of state, a peacock full of pride at his feet. Countess Frances wears Elizabethan dress, her hair swept back, with a cap and circlet, at her feet a wyvern. Countess Cecilia's dress is early Carolean in style. At her feet is a lion.

Their three children are included, Katherine at the head, the boys at the foot both holding skulls as symbols of their deaths. Known as the 'Witchcraft Tomb', the monument commemorates one of the best-known witchcraft trials in English history, described in detail by Michael Honeybone (2008). Part of the inscription reads, *"In 1608 he married ye lady Cecilia Hungerford, daughter to ye Honourable Knight Sir John Tufton, by whom he had two sons, both of which died in their infancy by wicked practises and sorcerye"*.

In 1598, Francis Manners had embarked on a 'grand tour' through France, Germany and Italy, culminating in a visit to the court of Rudolf II, Holy Roman Emperor. He was probably accompanied by the architect and theatre designer Inigo Jones amongst others. On his return, he joined his brothers Roger and George in the Essex rebellion. He was imprisoned as a consequence, and fined a thousand marks, but Robert Cecil obtained a remission of the fine probably as an act of reconciliation with the Essex faction. Like Roger, Francis was

The alabaster effigies of Francis Manners, 6th Earl of Rutland, and Countesses Frances (above the earl) and Cecilia (below).

reconciled on the accession of James I, and in 1605 took part in Prince Charles's investiture as Duke of York and was made a Knight of the Bath alongside the Prince.

On 26 June 1612 he became the 6th Earl of Rutland. Promotion to Lord Lieutenant of Lincolnshire followed as did the first of a series of visits by King James to Belvoir Castle. Francis played a part in the funeral of the King's eldest son, Henry Fredrick, Prince of Wales, on 6 November 1612, carrying a ceremonial shield. He again took a part in a ritual joust in 1613 to celebrate King James's accession day, carrying a shield bearing an *impresa* designed and painted by Shakespeare's leading actor Richard Burbage with a motto written by Shakespeare himself. Francis's steward recorded a payment *"to Mr Shakespeare in gold about my lord's impresa, 44s.; to Richard Burbage for painting and making it, in gold, 44s."*, one of William Shakespeare's few written records and much quoted by biographers.

Francis Manners married twice, firstly to Frances Kynvett with whom he had a daughter Katherine. With his second wife, Cecilia Hungerford, he had two sons, Henry and Francis, both of whom died in infancy of what the Earl believed was witchcraft, though a contemporary John Chamberlain described their condition as *the falling sickness*. Francis may have been influenced by King James, who particularly during his reign as James VI of Scotland was an enthusiastic witch hunter and had written a book, *Daemonologie* (1597), to counter a rational attack on the validity of witchcraft beliefs, Scot's *Discovery of Witchcraft*, which according to historian David Wootton was actually written in 1585 by Abraham Fleming, brother of the rector of Bottesford, Reverend Samuel Fleming. Abraham Fleming died in Bottesford in 1602 and is buried in St Mary's where his memorial brass plate can be seen in the floor before the altar steps. The king had ordered the *Discovery of Witchcraft*

Henry (left) and Francis Manners (right), the sons of the 6th Earl of Rutland and Countess Cecilia, both of whom were allegedly killed by witchcraft.

to be burned by the hangman on his accession, but seems to have tempered his belief toward the end of his reign. Nonetheless he probably exerted a powerful influence upon Francis, 6th Earl of Rutland. In 1619, three local women, Joan, Phillippa and Margaret Flower, were arrested for allegedly murdering Rutland's sons by witchcraft. All three lost their lives. Joan Flower reputedly died choking on bread she had asked for as a substitute for the Eucharist. Her two daughters were executed after their trial at Lincoln in 1619. Three other local women, Anne Baker of Bottesford, Joan Willimot of Goadby, and Ellen Greene of Stathern, were also arrested and examined, but their fate is not recorded.

Francis's daughter Katherine was selected by the Duchess of Buckingham to wed her son George Villiers, 1st Duke of Buckingham, the King's favorite and probable lover. However this did not go smoothly. The families were unable to agree the dowry and King James forbad his favourite from marrying a Catholic. Katherine, like her father, was a Catholic, but she eventually agreed to become a Protestant, the dowry was increased, and they married in 1620. They had four children before Buckingham's assassination in 1628 by a disaffected army officer, John Felton. In 1623, Francis had commanded the fleet accompanying Prince Charles back from Spain after the failure to gain the hand of the Spanish Infanta. This project, with its prospect of aligning the English and Spanish crowns during the Thirty Years War, horrified many of the English Protestants who would later come to be known as the Puritans. Their open celebration of its failure was one of the straws in the wind that foretold the conflicts to come. Francis Manners' last official duty was at James I's funeral in 1625. Katherine re-married the Irish peer Randal MacDonnell, 1st Marquis of Antrim, in 1635.

Effigy of Katherine, daughter of Francis, the 6th Earl of Rutland, and Countess Frances, his 1st wife, kneeling at the head of the tomb.

George Manners, 7th Earl of Rutland (1632 –1641).

Next to the priest's door, the neoclassical marble effigy of Earl George, standing erect in fanciful Roman dress. This tomb and that of the 8th Earl, both erected in 1686, were by Grinling Gibbons to designs by Gabriel Cibber. The Belvoir Accounts include a receipt dated 12th July, 1686, from Gibbons to the 9th Earl for £100 paid for two tombs. It seems that Earl George did not get his memorial until 45 years after his death.

The youngest son of the 4th Earl, George served in Ireland with his brothers Roger and Francis, and was knighted by the Earl of Essex. Like his brothers he joined the Essex Rebellion of 1601, but also like Francis was excused his fine after the intervention of Sir Robert Cecil. After the accession of James I he became MP for Grantham then in 1614 MP for Lincolnshire in the *Addled Parliament*, which tried but failed to limit James's extravagance. He served in the Parliament of 1621 and again in 1624 when he represented Stamford in the *Happy Parliament*, so called because it was James's last Parliament and was determined not to disagree with the king. Sir George Manners was re-elected in 1625 to the *Useless Parliament*, Charles I's first Parliament, which tried to limit the king's powers to raise customs duties in a way that no other monarch had previously experienced (Charles continued to raise customs revenue, and dismissed parliament when it tried to impeach Buckingham following his failure to lift the siege of La Rochelle). George Manners entered the peerage as the 7th Earl of Rutland in 1632 on the death of his brother Francis, and served in the Lords until his death in 1641, eighteen months before the start of the English Civil War. The Earl's wife, Countess Frances, daughter of Sir Edward Cary and sister of Viscount Falkland, the Royalist poet, died in 1641. They had no children and she was denied a place in this monument, which seems harsh and difficult to justify by modern standards. At any rate, his titles passed to his second cousin, John Manners.

Marble statue of George Manners, 7th Earl of Rutland.

John Manners, 8th Earl of Rutland (1641 – 1679) and Countess Frances (née Montague), d.1671.

Next to the vestry door is the white marble tomb of Earl John and Countess Frances, again in roman dress. He inherited after the death of the 7th Earl brought the direct descent to an end and the title passed to the cadet branch of Haddon Hall in Derbyshire. He was grandson of Sir John Manners of Haddon, who was the second son of Thomas, 1st Earl of Rutland. Countess Frances was the daughter of Edward Lord Montague of Boughton. They had at least eleven children. Of three sons only the third John survived, becoming the 9th Earl and, in 1703, 1st Duke of Rutland.

Earl John was MP for Derbyshire during the *Short Parliament* of 1640 and a supporter of Parliament. After inheriting in 1641 he sat in the House of Lords and was one of the few peers to remain in London despite the King's summons to Oxford after his failure to arrest the five Westminster MPs in 1642. Following the outbreak of the Civil War, Belvoir Castle was taken into Royalist possession by Gervase Lucas, a member of the Earl's household, and Baptist Noel, Viscount Campden (John Manners was later to claim compensation from the estate of Campden). The Castle became a Royalist cavalry base, visited by King Charles as well as Princes Rupert and Maurice. However, John Manners confirmed his loyalty to the Protestant cause in 1643 by signing the Solemn League and Covenant to install Presbyterian church government in

The marble effigies of John, 8th Earl of Rutland, and Countess Frances.

England in exchange for Scottish military support. The Castle was besieged in 1645 by Parliamentary soldiers under Sednham Poyntz, and Lucas surrendered on February 3rd, 1646, when he was allowed to march out with his garrison to Lichfield. The castle was demolished in 1649 with the reluctant agreement of the Earl of Rutland, as a part of the campaign to 'slight' or destroy English castles to prevent them being re-captured by the Royalists, as Colchester had been in the 2nd Civil War. Both Newark Castle and Nottingham Castle were slighted in the same process.

Faces of the marble statues of John Manners, the 8th Earl of Rutland, and Countess Frances.

John Manners served from 1646 as Chief Justice in Eyre, North of Trent. Like many Parliamentary leaders who later became Whigs he was reconciled to the Restoration of Charles II, becoming Lord Lieutenant of Leicestershire from 1667 until July 1677. Nichols reports that from 1666 he devoted most of his time to restoring Belvoir Castle. He died in 1679.

Stained Glass

The western window of the chancel clerestory contains reconstructed panels of medieval stained glass, the remains of the glass ejected from the nave during Victorian "restoration". Other windows of the chancel contain fine examples of Victorian stained and painted glass. The chancel is dominated by the east window by Thomas Willement, 'The Father of Victorian Stained Glass', dedicated " .... *To the Memory of Canon and Lady Adeliza Norman by the Parishioners and Friends December 1889*". In the south wall are two windows by Herbert Bryans, an associate of Charles Eamer Kempe. One commemorates " ... *A loving sister Lady Adeliza A.G. Norman*", who died in 1887, who was a sister of Charles, the 6th Duke of Rutland". The second, depicting "Faith Charity Hope", commemorates the 6th Duke himself, who died in 1888.

In the north wall, above the tomb of Lord John Roos, are two windows. The lower, by William Wailes, commemorates the death in 1874 of Richard Norman, elder son of Canon Frederick and Lady Adeliza Norman. The picture depicts Isaac and Abraham, but is more striking for the photographic quality of the portrait of the deceased as a child, mounted in the apex of the arch. The upper window, by Charles Eamer Kempe, with the words *"I am the Truth and the Light ...."*, commemorates Robert Manners Norman, the younger son, who succeeded his father as Rector in 1889 and died in 1895.

The south transept contains a magnificent example of Victorian stained-painted glass in its southern elevation. This depicts the Nativity surrounded by angels many playing medieval musical instruments. The central panels show the Holy Infant, Mary and Joseph flanked by the Shepherds and the Wise Men and accompanied by angels. This window commemorates the death in 1902 of Janetta, Countess of Rutland, a leading light in the Temperance Movement. It is attributed to the workshop of Charles Eamer Kempe, though his trademark wheatsheaf symbol is absent and the church inventory records the maker as Thomas Kempe. Above the Lady Chapel altar is the window with the inscription "Suffer little Children" dedicated to William Hickson, who died in 1883 aged 67. This window carries the signature of "Moore & Co Glass Printers London" , referring to A.L. Moore of Southampton Row.

The central part of the east window of the chancel.

Medieval stained glass *displayed in the SW window of the chancel clerestory. These are all that remains of what was once a large series located in the clerestory of the nave of St Mary's and described by Nichols (1795). The king is said to be St. Edward the Confessor, and bishop to be Leofric, Bishop of Exeter (1050—1072), though this is difficult to confirm. It is tragic that the remainder of the medieval windows at Bottesford were lost after Nichols' time, apparently during 'improvements' to the church.*

Victorian windows in the chancel of St Mary's.

Left: Part of the window erected in memory of Lady Adeliza Norman, d.1887, who was wife of Canon Frederick Norman and daughter of the 8th Duke of Rutland.

Centre: The roundel in the upper part of the lower of the two windows at the eastern end of the northern wall of the chancel. It contains a true portrait of Richard Norman (d.1874), the elder son of Canon Frederick Norman, who was Rector of Bottesford (1846— 1889) and Lady Adeliza Norman.

Right: the right-hand panel of the "Faith, Hope and Charity" window, commemorating Charles, the 8th Duke of Rutland, d.1888.

The Nativity window.

The south window in the Lady Chapel shows the Nativity and panels of angels, many playing a variety of medieval musical instruments. It is attributed to the workshop of Charles Eamer Kempe, the Late Victorian stained-glass maker, though it is admitted that his trademark sheaf of wheat emblem has not been located on this window.

The dedication written in the bottom-right panel reads, "To the glory of God in loving memory of Janetta Duchess of Rutland … 1902".

83

The Font - *detail of the carved panels of the octagonal Tudor font in St Mary's: probably dating from 1559-1563 (based on comments by Mr Harry Gill, writing in 1920).*

Two Rectors of Bottesford

Thomas White, Rector (1679-1685).

Thomas White, Bishop of Peterborough (1685), campaigned against the *Declaration of Indulgence* but was acquitted by James II in 1688, then was one of the *non-juring* bishops deprived of his see in 1690 by William and Mary. His memorial plaque is mounted on the east wall of the north transept, rather hidden behind the organ.

Henry de Codyngtoun, Rector of Bottesford (1361-1381).

The brass is noted for the rich embroidery on the cope depicting saints including Peter, Paul, John the Evangelist, Margaret, Catherine, Thomas of Canterbury and James of Compostela.

Glossary

alabaster - fine-grained white or lightly-tinted variety of gypsum, used ornamentally

bestiary - a medieval treatise of real and/or imaginary animals.

cap-of-maintenance - a ceremonial cap of crimson velvet lined with ermine, worn on top of the helmet and blazoned with the family's crest.

chantry - an endowment or chapel for the maintenance of a priest to sing a daily mass for the souls of specified people.

clerestory - the upper part of a wall containing windows to let in natural light to the nave, transept or choir of a church or cathedral.

corbel - a bracket jutting from a wall to carry a weight such as a roof timber.

cruciform - cross-shaped.

green man - carved figure with foliage sprouting from his mouth, sometimes believed to represent a pre-Christian fertility figure.

hauberk - a shirt of mail usually reaching at least to mid-thigh and including sleeves.

hood-mould - a strip of protruding stonework surrounding the upper parts of a window or doorway.

label-stop - a carving located at the end of a hood-mould.

Liassic ironstone - iron-rich limestone from the Liassic geological period.

Middle Jurassic oolitic-limestone ashlar - high-quality pinkish grey limestone building stone of Middle Jurassic geological age.

mullion - a vertical bar between the casements of a window.

orle - the wreath or chaplet surmounting or encircling the helmet of a knight and bearing the crest.

piscina - wall-niche with sink for washing sacramental vessels with holy water.

rood screen - decorated screen between chancel and nave surmounted by a large carved crucifix (the rood).

springer - a stone at the base of an arch from which the arch springs.

tilt-heaume - a helmet worn during tilting (jousting) at tournaments.

Bibliography

Dare, M.P. 1950. *The Story of St. Mary the Virgin, Bottesford, Leics. And its monuments.* The British Publishing Company, Gloucester.

David Start and David Stocker (editors) 2011, *Making of Grantham the medieval town.* Heritage Trust for Lincolnshire.

The Duchess of Rutland and Pruden, J. 2009. *Belvoir Castle*, Frances Lincoln Ltd, London.

Esdaile, Andrew 1845. *Esdaile's Rutland Monuments: with a description of Bottesford church and parish*. Reprinted by Kessinger [*www.kessinger.net*] .

Honeybone, M. 2008. *Wicked Practise and Sorcerye, The Belvoir Witchcraft case of 1619*. Baron Books, Buckingham.

McClure, N.E. (editor) 1939. *The Letters of John Chamberlain.* Philadelphia.

Gililov, Ilya 2003. *The Shakespeare Game: the mystery of the Great Phoenix*. Angora Publishing.

Gill, Harry 1920. *The Church of St Mary, Orston*. Transactions of the Thoroton Society, Vol.XXIV, pp. 39-49.

Lovejoy, Arthur O. 1936. *The Great Chain of Being*. Harvard University Press.

Nichols, John 1975. *History and Antiquities of Leicestershire and Rutland,* Volume II, Part 1, 1795.

Oxford University Press. *Oxford Dictionary of National Biography* (articles on the lives of the Earls of Rutland).

Pevsner, Nikolaus revised by Elizabeth Williamson 1984. *The Buildings of England, Leicestershire and Rutland*. 2nd Edition, pp.105-108.

Shipman, E.A. 1992. *The Church of St Mary the Virgin, Bottesford, Leicestershire.* Bottseford Parochial Church Council (out of print).

Shipman, E.A. 1995. *Gleanings about the Church of St Mary the Virgin, Bottesford, Leicestershire*. Published privately (out of print).

Woodcock, Alex 2011. *Gargoyles and Grotesques*. Shire Publications, Oxford.

Wootton, David 2001. *Reginald Scot / Abraham Fleming / The Family of Love.* in *Languages of witchcraft*. ed. / Stuart Clark. New York : St. Martin's Press, pp. 119-39.